EASINGTON LIFEBOAT

1913 – 1933

A HISTORY

by

Mike Welton

Easington
SKEALS 2010

Copyright: Mike Welton

ISBN 978-0-9565048-0-7

Front cover: photo of the *Docea Chapman* returning after a launch, and a picture of the crew in 1922

Back cover: photos of a model of the boat and boat house

ILLUSTRATIONS

Introduction page: The lifeboat shed in 1963, showing just how much land has been eroded by the sea

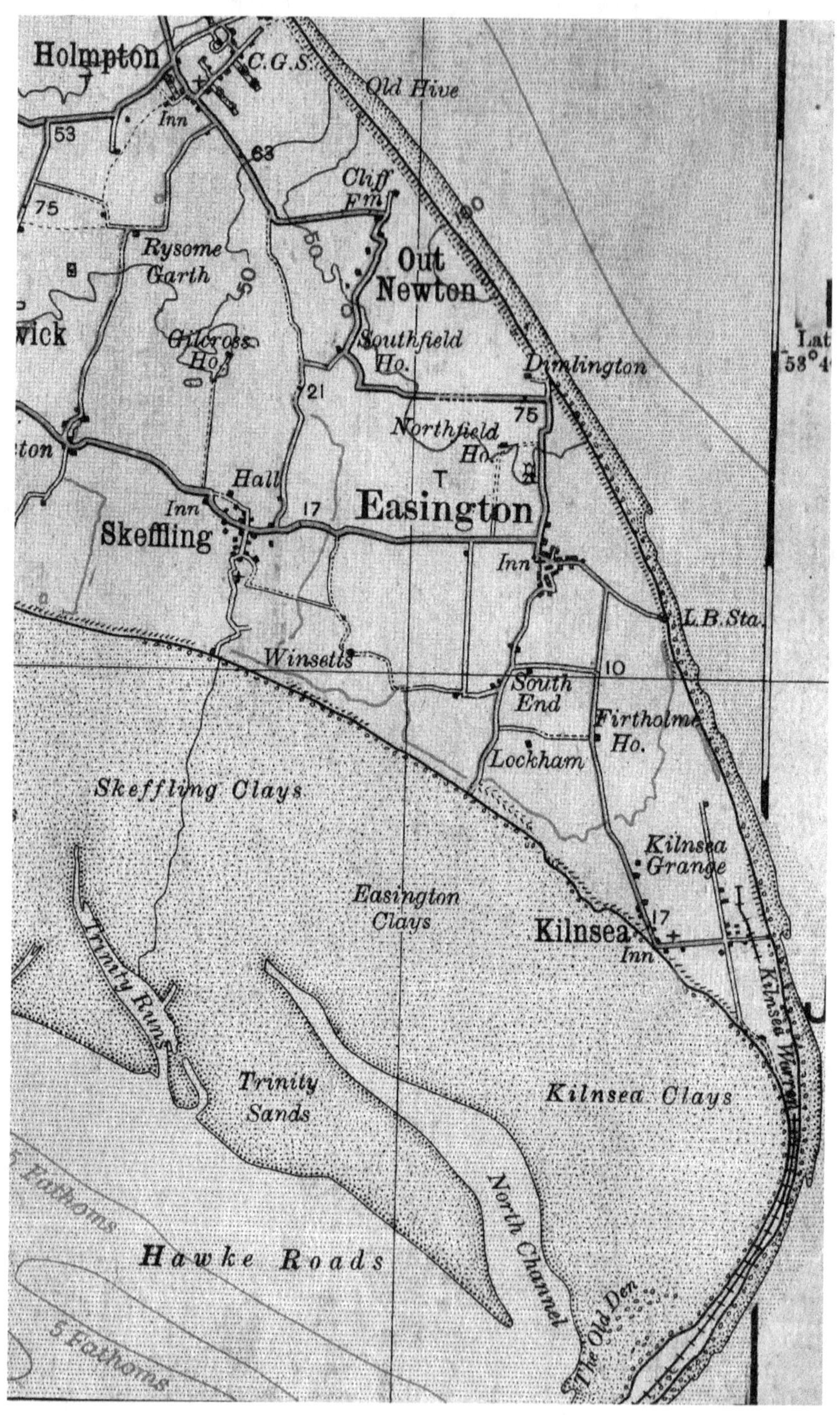

Holmpton
C.G.S.
Old Hive
Inn
53
63
75
Cliff Fm
Rysome Garth
50
Out Newton
Gilcross Ho.
Southfield Ho.
wick
Dimlington
Lat 53°4'
21
Northfield Ho.
75
ton
Hall
Easington
Inn
Skeffling
17
Inn
L.B.Sta.
Winsetts
South End
10
Firtholme Ho.
Lockham
Skeffling Clays
Kilnsea Grange
Easington Clays
Kilnsea
17
Inn
Kilnsea Warren
Trinity Runs
Trinity Sands
Kilnsea Clays
Fathoms
North Channel
Hawke Roads
The Old Den
5 Fathoms

Introduction

It is now 100 years since the Easington Lifeboat, *DOCEA CHAPMAN*, was built, and 77 years since it left the village after a 20-year spell of life-saving duties. There is nothing left of the original lifeboat shed base that had teetered on the cliff edge for so many years.

The lifeboat shed pictured in 1963, some distance from the cliff edge

This is an updated version and revised publication of a book that was produced in 2003, now with some additional photographs and information. With the previous book I was assisted by Larry Malkin with the compilation, and the late Norman Clarke with its production on his computer, and I acknowledge their help. Thanks also to Peter and Jan Crowther for proof reading and preparing the book for publication.

This present book is published by SKEALS (Spurn, Kilnsea, and Easington Area Local Studies Group). I hope this records the history of the lifeboat and its crews, so it will not be lost from memory forever.

DOCEA CHAPMAN

The Easington Lifeboat

The lifeboat stationed at Easington, near Spurn Point, in East Yorkshire, was a rowing, self-righting 'Rubie' type, thirty four feet in length, with an eight-foot beam and a drop keel. She would normally carry a crew of thirteen men, ten of whom were oarsmen. She was numbered 623, and was built in 1910, by the Thames Ironworks in London, at a cost of £830.

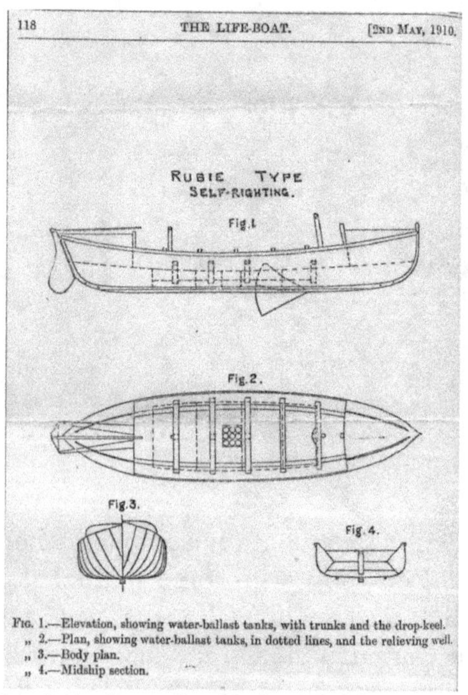

Fig. 1 A plan of a 'Rubie' lifeboat 1910

She was named *Docea Chapman* in memory of the wife of the main benefactor, Mr Joseph Chapman, a timber merchant of Great Grimsby in Lincolnshire. His wife, Docea, had died in March 1891 in Zurich, Switzerland, and is buried there.

*Fig. 2 Docea Chapman's headstone in St. Michael's churchyard
at Little Coates, Lincolnshire: a replica of the one in Zurich*

Joseph died in London May 1909, aged 69 years.

Fig. 3 Newspaper cutting from The Grimsby News

He is buried in St. Michael's churchyard at Little Coates, Lincolnshire.

Fig. 4 Joseph Chapman's tomb

The boat was originally stationed at Withernsea, a town seven miles north of Easington, from December 8th 1911, until the station closed on May 29th 1913, because extra coastal-protection groynes, had rendered the launching of the boat extremely hazardous at certain states of the tide. The long-shore drift on this part of the coastline could have carried the boat down onto the sea defences, and seriously endangered the crew. Other reasons for the move were the recent lighting of the Withernsea lighthouse, which gave more adequate warning of the town to mariners, and the modern construction of boats in iron, which helped to save lives because vessels no longer broke into pieces as they were stranded. Whilst stationed at Withernsea records tell us that the boat was launched three times on service but no lives were saved.

Launched 10th January 1912 — no service.

Launched 2nd December 1912 — no service.

Launched 3rd December 1912 —Trawler *Rhodesia* of Grimsby - helped save vessel.

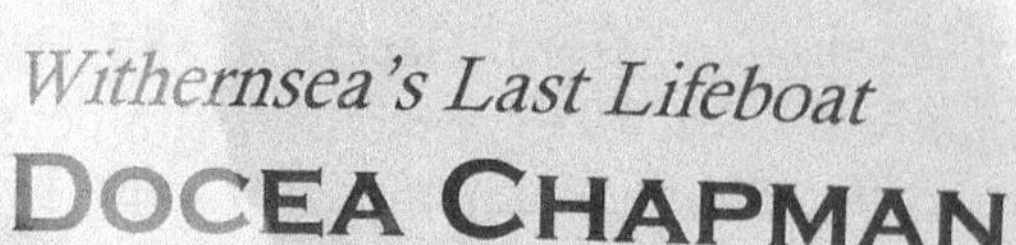

Fig. 5 Information board in Withernsea Lighthouse museum

Fig. 6 The Withernsea Lifeboat prior to re-naming

On February the 13th 1913, the committee of the Royal National Lifeboat Institution (RNLI) decided that a Deputy Chief Inspector should visit Easington and report on the desirability of establishing a lifeboat station at a lane end that led from the village. The Inspector did not report back until May 8th of that year, the recommendation being the moving of the *Docea Chapman* to a new station, nearer the mouth of the River Humber.

The committee accepted the proposals and recommended that the Withernsea station be closed and the lifeboat be transferred 'experimentally' to Easington. The lifeboat house at Withernsea was to be retained until the question of making Easington a permanent station was settled.

The committee also instructed the District Inspector to select an Honorary Secretary, enrol a crew, arrange for the provision of horses to assist in launching and recovery, and obtain an estimate for the construction of a wooden or corrugated iron shed for the stores, together with permission for its erection, and for the lifeboat carriage to stand on the selected site.

On May 30th 1913 the boat was brought from Withernsea by road with a team of horses and officially came on station on May 31st 1913. The 'experiment' appeared to have been a success for the boat was to remain in the village for a further twenty years, being placed into the reserve fleet in July 1933, until sold in 1939.

The RNLI minutes of June 12th 1913 reported that the lifeboat and carriage withdrawn from Withernsea had been stationed at Easington 'experimentally', the boat being 'sheeted down' on the cliff top on common land. There was great regret at the departure of the boat from Withernsea, through surprisingly she was not received with much enthusiasm from Easington people. In fact the RNLI District Inspector reported that he had visited the station to receive the boat and found that the local fishermen and village inhabitants "did not want anything to do with her". However following a public meeting, all but three fishermen agreed to crew the new boat and others volunteered to act as helpers. Following the meeting, the lifeboat was satisfactorily launched and beached, but there were problems with the untrained horses. This was apparently so serious that the District Inspector proposed that launching by hand would be more desirable until extra horse training could be undertaken. In his report the Inspector also stated that the lifeboat stood on common land, so that there was no necessity to obtain permission for her to remain there

On November 13th 1913, the Easington Rector, Reverend Walter Holt, was appointed Honorary Secretary. In reports the District Inspector told of a difficulty caused by the Coxswain, Robert Little, having to absent himself in connection with fishing out of Grimsby. It was felt that he was the only man fit to hold the post, the second Coxswain being only 22 years of age. In order to overcome the problem the committee decided that Robert Little be asked to give up his fishing for the coming winter and be compensated for remaining in the village in charge of the lifeboat at a cost of £10 per quarter or £20 for the season. Robert Little originally accepted the offer but then suffered a change of heart and left in December 1913.

Fig. 7 The Lifeboat crew of 1913
L. to R. unknown, Jack Stevenson, unknown, Dod Hopper, Geo. Stevenson Jnr., Herbert Marritt, Jack Pinder, Geo. Stevenson Snr., Geo Brown, Fred Hopper, unknown, Mr. Robert Walker

Fig. 8 Lifeboat Crew
With the Rev. W. Holt (Hon Sec.) seated front right. The four men
in uniform would have been Board of Trade Coastguards

In January 1914 the District Inspector reported to the RNLI that
the coxswain, Robert Little, was unable to accept the offer to
compensate him for remaining in Easington for the winter period.
His lack of enthusiasm for the boat was not now shared by the rest
of his fellow villagers, for there had been a "change in the spirit of
the local men" and there was a new general desire to form a crew
and work the boat. A new coxswain, Herbert Marritt, had been
appointed as well as a new bowman (Herbert Marritt successfully
continued to hold the post from December 1913 to December
1916). The positive support led to another report in May 1914,
when the Inspector reported very favourably on the experimental
station at Easington, and asked the Chief Inspector to visit the
station with a view to erecting a permanent boathouse and station
on the cliff top.

At their committee meeting in July 1914 the members considered
the Chief Inspector's report and recommendations which were:-
1. That the Easington Parish Council be asked to grant a lease of a
site for the proposed boathouse on waste land at the side of the
main road for a nominal rent.

2. That the engineers visit Easington and prepare a site plan and specification of a corrugated iron boathouse.

3. That the Parish Council be asked for permission to widen the fishermen's gap to a width of 20 foot and cut it back to a gradient of about 1 in 6 feet.

4.That subject to the permission of the owner, the gates and gap between the fields leading from the main road to the cliffs at Neville's Farm be widened and that a passage to the beach of 20 foot wide be considered.

The proposals were duly put before Easington Parish Council on September 21st 1914. The minutes of the meeting show that H. Clubley moved that 'Permission be given to the National Lifeboat Institution to erect a boat shed in 10 Chains Lane as indicated on place 810' (produced)'. The motion was seconded by W. Curtis. CARRIED.

The meeting continued:-
Moved by J.Harrison, Seconded by H.J. Marritt:
"That the sum of 5 shillings be charged for the site as a loss of the sale of herbage". CARRIED.

Moved by J.Clubley, Seconded by J. Harrison:
"That this Council have no objection to the above named Institution widening the slope to the sea shore indicated on place 810B". CARRIED.

On November the 12th 1914 the RNLI committee approved tenders for work at the boathouse amounting to £1,047 and for widening 'Fishermen's Gap' amounting to £110. The boathouse itself, constructed in wood and corrugated iron, was of typical design having a rounded roof, wash down and drainage facilities and large opening doors at either end. The east end of the boathouse was of a two-storey construction, the upper deck consisting of a room for use as a crew room and office. The building was completed in 1915.

Fig. 9 The lifeboat shed viewed from the west

Fig. 10 The shed viewed from the sea side (east)

Fig. 11 A painting of the lifeboat shed by Vera Addison in 1923

During 1914 the lifeboat was launched twice on service, first on the 28th of March to the Grimsby trawler *Minotaur*, when she stood by the vessel, and secondly to the Grimsby steam trawler *Ipswich*, when she rescued six trawlermen. No doubt there was much rejoicing in the village at the first successful launching of their lifeboat.

In February 1916 the District Inspector reported that the arrangements in the new boathouse were excellent and also that the coastguards, except in very exceptional circumstances, could fill any possible vacancies in the crew. This was an important statement, for at this time the country had been at war with Germany for two years and recruitment of local men would have been significant. Many of the local men would have been called away to the Flanders trenches and service in the Royal and Merchant navies, which were under great pressure from the German 'U' boat menace.

The situation grew worse before it got better, for in December 1916 the Inspector reported that a crew had not been available for the previous exercise on November 1st, and that the boat had not

18

been exercised at all in the previous summer. This was a grave concern, for at this time enemy submarines were very active on this coast and the lifeboat could be called out at any time to rescue the crew of a torpedoed boat or one that had been damaged by gunfire. The Inspector assured the committee however, that should the boat be required for service, a crew could be found.

The situation became slightly easier in January 1917, when a new coxswain, John Henry Branton, was appointed. John Henry held the position until December 1931, and seemed able to raise sufficient men to crew the boat, according to reports on July 6th 1917 and again on April 11th 1919, when more men would be available as hostilities against Germany had ceased the year before, and discharged soldiers and sailors were returning home.

Fig. 12 Coxswain Jack Henry Branton (on the right) pictured with Ned Curtis

It was not only men that were needed to launch and man the boat. Horses too were needed, to haul the boat and its carriage down to the water. The 'Rubie' type needed ten of these animals, which at Easington were supplied by local farmers. When a launch was imminent the crew first contacted Henry Clubley of Dimlington Farm, who usually supplied six horses and Blashills at Low Farm, and Granthams at Rail Hall Farm, who contributed the rest. It must have taken some time to assemble these beasts in an emergency, especially if they were engaged in fieldwork at the far end of the farm.

Fig. 13 The horses pulling the lifeboat

Fig. 14 Bringing the boat down through Fishermen's Gap onto the beach prior to launching

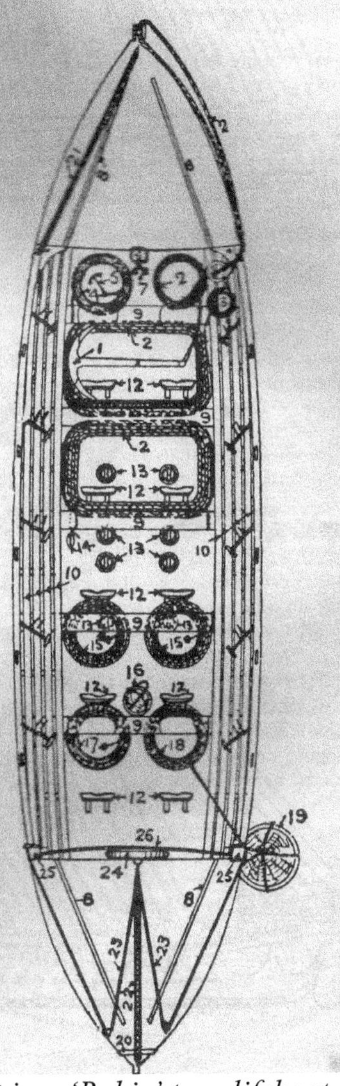

Fig. 15 *The layout of equipment in a 'Rubie' type lifeboat*

Fig. 16 On the beach, the wheels of the carriage had sand tracks known as 'tipping plates' so that the wheels did not bury themselves in the sand

Launching

On launching, the boat and carriage were taken out into sufficient depth of water and the team brought round to the right, to end up facing the beach, with the lifeboat now directed at the sea, ready for launching. Ropes were passed round blocks on the carriage, and when the Coxswain, who was studying the pattern of the waves, judged it right, he would give the order, the helpers would pull on the ropes and the lifeboat would shoot forward.

At the same time the crew would take their first stroke into the oncoming wave and if all went well the boat would be on its way.

However, if the command was given too soon, the breaking wave would turn the boat broadside onto the sea or beach and possibly roll her over, endangering both crew and helpers. Timing was crucial to the exercise and this where the skill and experience of the Coxswain played its part. One second too early or too late and the rescuers could end up having to be rescued themselves.

Fig. 17 Hauling the boat out into position

*Fig. 18 Positioning the boat ready for the launch,
oars at the ready*

Fig. 19 Helpers man the ropes

At a later date the procedure was changed slightly, when the two lead horses were engaged to pull the launching ropes, as opposed to them being pulled by hand. This obviously reduced the danger to the helpers but increased it to the lead horses and their riders, who had to be very experienced indeed to handle the animals in the treacherous breakers.

On one occasion the handling skills were not good enough, when the team broke to the left and not the right as was customary. This turn took the lifeboat into an area known as 'Clay Huts', where the sea had worn numerous deep gullies into the old forest bed of boulder clay, making it an easy location for man or horse to slip. This in fact, is what happened and the boat almost turned over onto the launching crew. Fortunately good horse handling skills saved the day, and disaster was narrowly averted. Incidentally the instructions for the horses to turn right were "Gee" and for going left "Hove".

Fig. 20 Horse down at the 'Clay Huts'

Fig. 21 Trying to rescue the horse

Eye witnesses have told how the horses would scream as they became afraid in deep water, and untrained horses must have been very difficult to control in rough water.

In order to overcome the horse's natural fear of the water, and to ensure the success of a lifeboat launch, in the event of a ship in distress, practice launchings took place four times a year, when a crew could be raised. Two of these took place in summer and two in winter. On each occasion the crew received five shillings and sixpence (27p) for the summer launch and nine shillings and sixpence (48p) for the winter, and the launching team and horse handlers also received a nominal sum. The small amount for the launching crew increased if they got wet, and one particular person in the crew always did, even if it meant throwing himself down into the surf!

26

Fig. 22 The crew of the lifeboat in 1922 with Rev. Holt, Hon. Sec. seated front left, with Mr. Robert Walker seated next to him.

Fig. 23 A bit of maintenance

Recovering the Boat

To recover the boat, it would be brought in as near to the shore as possible, then hauled by hand and by horse across the beach using wooden skids. These would be placed in front of the boat and as it moved over them they would be removed and brought around again. There was also a device that consisted of two rollers in a wooden block that sat upon a small turn-table. The keel of the boat would be positioned and balanced on the rollers. It could then be rotated to line up with the boat carriage and then hauled on to the carriage and secured.

Fig. 24 Hauling the boat out of the water using wooden skids to drag it over the sand

Fig. 25 Horses dragging the boat ashore

Fig. 26 Photo taken from a model, showing the beach skids and the device for hauling the boat to be able to position it to put it back on the carriage

*Fig. 27 Part of the original lifeboat equipment, the keel turn-table
used for placing the boat back on the carriage*

*Fig. 28 The turn-table device used for lining the up the boat
(Lynmouth Museum)*

Fig. 29 Hauling the boat back up the slipway at Fishermen's Gap. The fishermen's huts can be seen in the background

The crew itself consisted of thirteen men, Coxswain, 2nd Coxswain, Bowman and ten oarsmen. The man immediately in front of the Coxswain facing him was known as the 'Stroke Oar' and the other oarsman took their timing from him. Any new man was known as 'Rookie Oar', and he was always placed to the rear of the team at the bows of the boat, where he could do least harm and in case he missed the stroke or the water and fell over backwards!

Attached to the side of the boat, at each oarsman's place was a line of cork floats. This line was placed over the rower's knees when at sea, so that if they went overboard, or capsized they would have something to hang on to. The Coxswain and 2nd Cox had a line rigged at the helm position and the Bowman had a line fixed to the board head in the bows.

Fig. 30 A painting of the Easington lifeboat by Alf Duck, an Easington resident

In the event of being at sea for a prolonged period, the lifeboat had a ration box, which contained a few basic provisions. This could be used after sixteen hours at sea, which could easily happen if the boat had to 'Stand By' a vessel in difficulties. However this was not good enough for crewman Bob Wilson on one occasion! He could not wait for the sixteen hours to go by, whilst on service to the Grimsby trawler *Sea Lion* off Dimlington Observer Post on the 2nd April 1933. After a while he unscrewed the hasp of the locked provision box and helped himself to rum and chocolate, before replacing the hasp and screwing it back in place. After the crime, an enquiry was held and George Curtis (Coxswain from January 1932 until the removal of the boat in July 1933) had some rather tricky explaining to do!

On another occasion whilst out on a launch, a mouse emerged out of a life jacket, having made a home there in the kapok filling, whilst it was stored in the boathouse racks.

It would appear that George Curtis did not always enjoy marital bliss and on one or two occasions he had cause to spend the night in the upper crew room of the lifeboat shed. On one of the times he was so accommodated, he spotted flares sent up by the vessel *Bravo*. The crew assembled and the lifeboat launched to assist, but in the event the boat managed without the crew of the *Docea Chapman* and the lifeboat returned on station without action.

A similar event resulted in a rather more embarrassing situation for the troubled husband. Whilst again sheltering in his roost, he failed to be aroused by flares sent up by the Herring Drifter *Autumn*, which eventually washed ashore by herself, a little further south towards Spurn. The crew abandoned ship and waded ashore before walking to the Blue Bell Inn at Kilnsea, the next village along the coast. No doubt George Curtis received some humorous comments from his crew after his peaceful slumber throughout the incident.

Another unsubstantiated story tells of the Easington boat being launched in heavy spray and surf to assist a vessel that was in difficulties, in daytime, to the south of the village. After a great struggle against the tide, the lifeboat came up to the stern of the distressed vessel, and the Coxswain attempted to make contact with the survivors. Much to the consternation of the lifeboat crew their attempts were met with silence and after a long wait the boat rowed sadly back to Easington, thinking that the wrecked sailors had been swept overboard to certain death in the tumbling seas. In fact, what the lifeboat crew could not see through the tremendous spray was that the bows of the beached boat, were already on the beach, and the crew had jumped off, and walked to safety in much the same way as the crew of the *Autumn*. Whilst the story may be apocryphal, it does give some idea of the difficulties that the Easington boat had in the tricky tides and seas that can occur on this lee coastline.

Easington Lifeboat Crew – 1920s

Fig. 31 Silhouette outline of crew members (see Fig. 32)

1.Fred Hopper
2. Billy Boyd
3. George Curtis
4. Vicar Holt
5. Dod Hopper
6. Bob Wilson
7. Jim Biglin
8. Alan Douglas
9. Castle Carrick
10. Redvers Clubley
11. Walt Biglin
12. Wally Clubley
13. Harry Goundrill
14. Arthur Garsides

Fig. 32 Photo of the crew

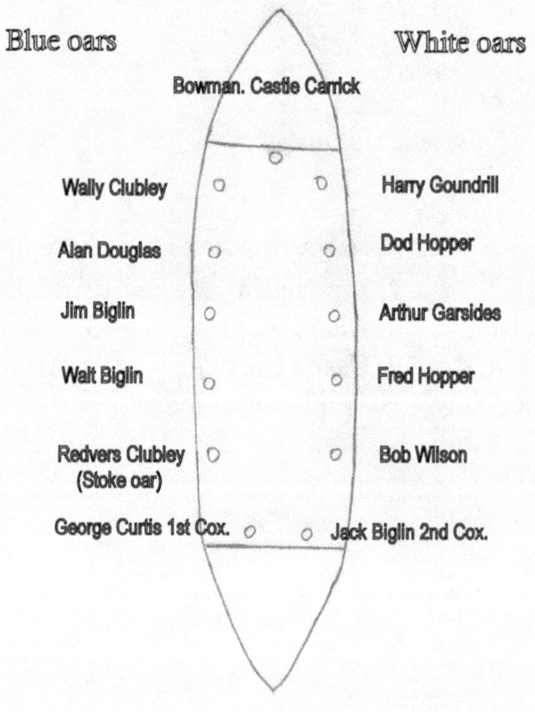

Fig. 33 Positions of crew members

Fig. 34 Easington Lifeboat Crew and fishermen assisting with the salvage operations of the wreck of Lucerne in 1929

Back Row L. to R.–
Pomp Carrick, Wally Clubley, Harry Goundrill, Herbert Marritt, George Stevenson, 'Clubley, 'unknown', 'unknown', Dod Hopper, 'unknown', 'unknown, Redvers Clubley.

Front Row L. to R. –
Walt Biglin, Reg Clubley, Jack Biglin, Jack Stevenson, 'unknown'.

Fig. 35 Photo of horses involved with the lifeboat and salvage work on the beach

<u>List of Coxswains of the *Docea Chapman*</u>:

Robert Little – May 1913 to December 1913
Henry Marritt – December 1913 to December 1916
John Henry Branton – January 1917 to December 1931
George Curtis – January 1932 to July 1933

<u>The Hon.Secretaries were:</u>
Rev. C. M. Barnes – 1913
Rev. Walter Holt – 1913 to 1932
Rev. A. L. Robbins – 1932 to 1933

Sadly, no medals were awarded to the Easington Station, but from a total of sixteen launches twenty eight lives were saved in nine successful rescues. This is no mean record for the crew and villagers that served. Though at first reluctant to take on the responsibility of the boat, they soon responded to the call of duty, as brave men and women will do, every time!

In the early nineteen-thirties Inspector Carver was replaced by Lieut. Commander P. E. Vaux. This gentleman came down to Easington with a view to closing the station, due mainly to the fact that in the opinion of the RNLI the new Humber Lifeboat, *City of Bradford II*, stationed at Spurn Point, was powerful enough and fast enough to cover the whole area. A meeting to assess local feeling was held in the Church Hall and the argument was that if the Humber Lifeboat was called out on service and another call for assistance occurred, there would be no cover available locally. This argument won the day and the lifeboat received a reprieve.

However this could not last and the end of an era came to pass in 1933. On May 5th of that year the *Hull Daily Mail* stated:-

"Easington villagers are viewing with dismay the prospect of an early closing down of their lifeboat station. They have been notified that their lifeboat the *DOCEA CHAPMAN* will shortly be taken away, and as there is no promise of a replacement the long and honorable connection with Easington and the lifeboat service is almost at an end. Such a position is purely in accord with the march of the times. The Easington Lifeboat has served its day and generation extremely well, but now nears its end as a much more modern type of craft – the Spurn motor lifeboat – can easily cover that portion of the coast which was Easington's preserve".

50 years ago

FROM the Hull Daily Mail of May 5, 1933.

EASINGTON villagers are viewing with dismay the prospect of an early closing down of their lifeboat station. They have been notified that their lifeboat, the Dorcea Chapman, will shortly be taken away, and as there is no promise of a replacement, the long and honourable connection of Easington with the lifeboat service is almost at an end.

Such a position is purely in accord with the march of the times. the Easington lifeboat has served its day and generation extremely well, but now nears its end as a much more modern type of craft — the Spurn motor lifeboat — can easily cover that portion of the coat which was Easington's preserve.

Fig. 36 A cutting from the Hull Daily Mail

*Fig. 37   Docea Chapman leaving Easington,
June 7th 1933*

Fig. 38 The lifeboat on its way to Patrington railway station

The lifeboat shed at Easington survived until 1969, when it was dismantled. Even the base of the shed has now disappeared, being taken away by the ever-encroaching sea on this swiftly eroding coastline. All that remains of this fine service in the area are the memories in the minds of villagers and the service boards, which are situated in the Lighthouse Museum at Withernsea, after their restoration by a previous Spurn Lifeboat Coxswain, the late Mr. Robertson Buchan.

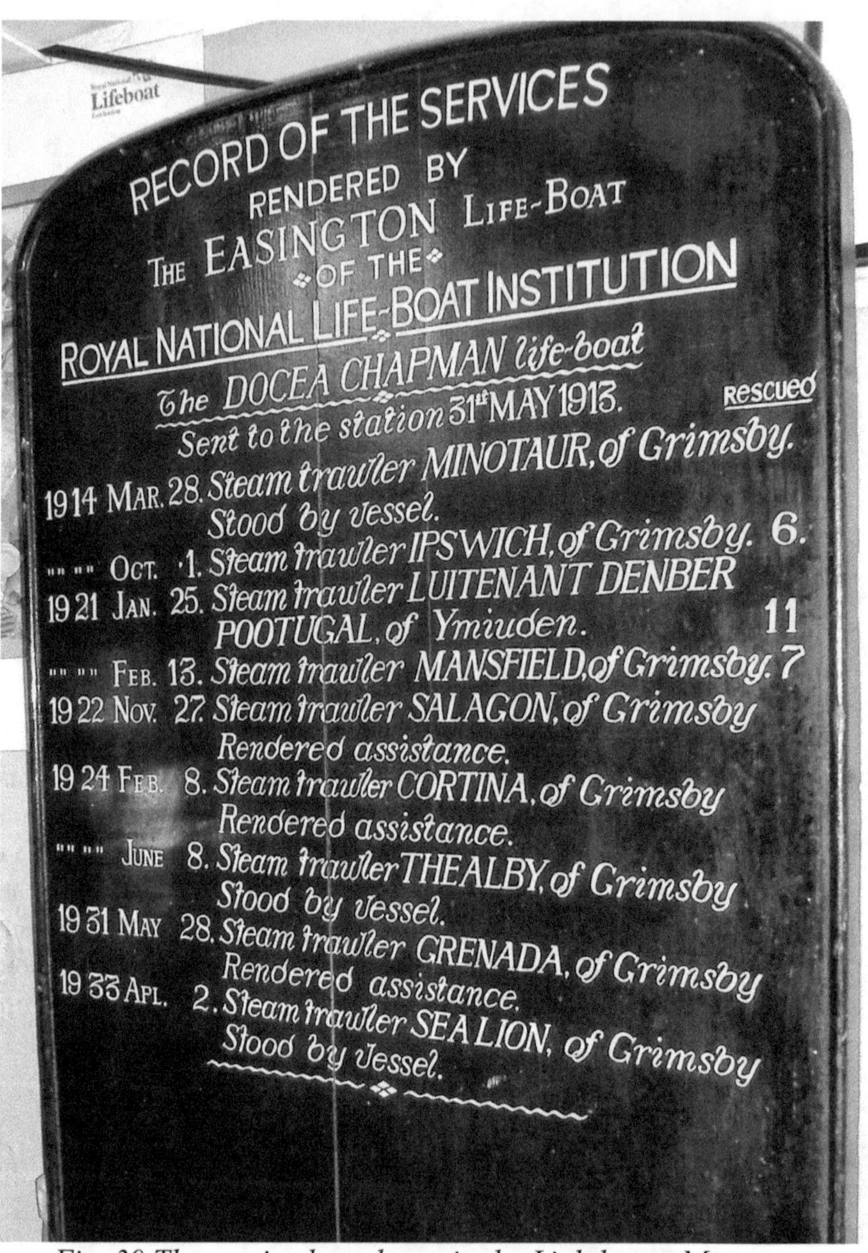

Fig. 39 The service board now in the Lighthouse Museum, Withernsea

Fig. 40 The shed base in 1981

Fig. 41 The base in 1987

Fig. 42 The base in 1988

Fig. 43 The War Memorial

Although the shed base has now disappeared, some of the unusual blue floor bricks have survived and been put to good use, seen here as part of the Easington War Memorial. They can also be seen in other parts of the village as garden paths.

Fig. 44 A garden path with lifeboat house bricks

Fig. 45 Even the old boat shed doors have been given a new home

List of all service launches by **DOCEA CHAPMAN**

Date	Vessel and service	Lives saved
1914-March 28th	S.T. *MINOTAUR* of Grimsby	Stood by vessel
1914-Oct 1st	S.T. *IPSWICH* of Grimsby	Rescued Persons - 6
1919-Oct 10th	An unknown steamer	No service
1919-Dec 12th	S.T. *REGAL* of Grimsby	No service
1921- Jan 25th	S.T. *LUITENANT DEN BEER PORTUGAL* of Ymuiden	Rescued Persons - 11
1921-Feb13th	S.T. *MANSFIELD* of Grimsby	Rescued Persons - 4
1922-Nov 27th	S.T. *SALAGON* of Grimsby	Rescued Persons - 7
1922-Nov 30th	S.T. *ISERNIA* of Grimsby	No service
1924- Feb 8th	S.T. *CORTINA* of Grimsby	Rendered assistance
1924- June 8th	S.T. *THEALBY* of Grimsby	Stood by vessel
1926-July 8th	S.T. *TREASURE* of Grimsby	No service
1927-Feb 17th	S.T. *PANDORA* of Hull	No service
1929-Dec 17th	S.T. *LUCERNE* of Grimsby	No service
1929-Dec 17th	S.T. *BENGAL* of Grimsby	No service
1931- May 28th	S.T. *GRENADA* of Grimsby	Rendered assistance
1933- April 2nd	S.T. *SEA LION* of Grimsby	Stood by vessel

TOTAL LIVES SAVED – 28

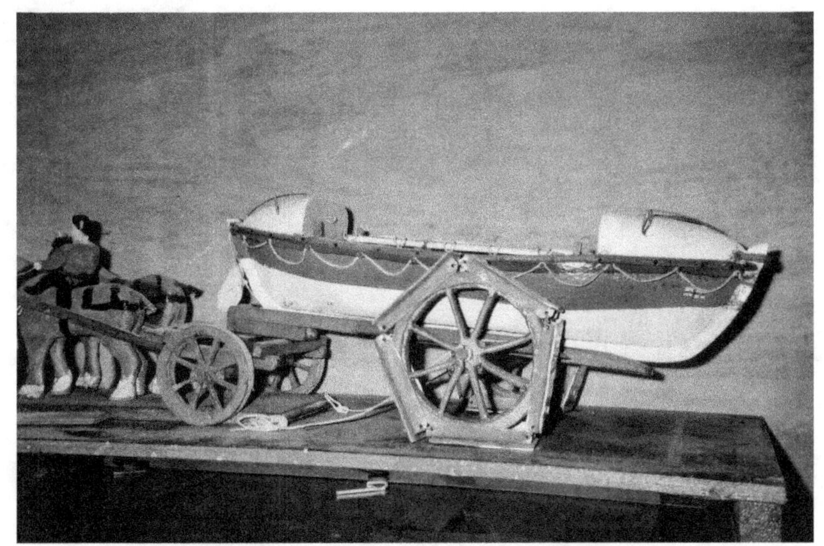

Fig. 46 Photos of a model of the Easington lifeboat with crew and horses made by the late Mr. Harry Ellarby

Fig. 47 The model by Mr. Harry Ellarby

Fig. 48 Mr Harry Ellarby with his model

Extracts from the Diary of Mr. R. W. Walker of the Tower House, Easington, Chairman of the Lifeboat Committee from November 1913 to April 1929.

1913
May 29th   Easington made a lifeboat station.
Nov 12th   Lifeboat meeting held in the schoolroom at which I was chairman. I was also elected Chairman of the Committee.
Dec 6th   Lifeboat practice under Captain Hall and a committee meeting in this house [Tower House].
Dec 20th   Lifeboat practice.
1914
March 26th   Lifeboat practice with Captain Rigg. I went out with them for the first time. Afterwards had a committee meeting.
June 18th   Captain Rigg and Commander Holmes were at Easington about lifeboat shed.
1915
March 20th   Lifeboat practice. I went out with it.
Oct 30th   Was at lifeboat launch 2 p.m. paid 1/-

1916

Jan 18th   Lifeboat practice with Inspector Hoyle R.N. and I went out with them.

1917

June 4th   Lifeboat practice with Inspector Hoyle .

Oct 27th   Lifeboat practice, but could not launch. Very heavy surf rolling in at high water. Got very wet.

Dec 27th   Lifeboat practice with Inspector Hoyle. Went out with them. Rough.

1919

Feb 3rd   At a lifeboat committee meeting in Institute.

Feb 22nd   Lifeboat practice with Inspector Hoyle and I and Lieut. Robinson went out.

Dec 17th   Lifeboat went out at 6a.m. beyond Dimlington high land and then to Kilnsea.

1920

April 24th   Lifeboat committee meeting in the boat house with Commander Carver, the Inspector, present.

1921

Jan 25th   About 6:30 p.m. the Dutch S.T. *Lieutenant General De Beer Poortugaal* came ashore near the Park. The rocket cart out. Saw the lifeboat launched and she brought ashore 14 men who had left the trawler in their boat, which they had abandoned.

Feb 13th   The S.T. *Mansfield* of Grimsby came ashore at 7 a.m. at Dimlington High land. Our lifeboat out and took off 4 men, and the rocket cart 5 men. The *Mansfield* towed off about 7:30 p.m.

June 18th   Lifeboat practice and I went out with them.

Dec 11th   S.T. *Kedworthy Castle* of Swansea came ashore at road end about 2:30 a.m.. Lifeboat and rocket cart out but neither used. Towed off about 1.30 a.m.

Dec 31st   Lifeboat practice, but I did not go to it. Boat failed to get off.

1922

Jan 28th S.T. *Acuba* of Grimsby came ashore at Dimlington High Ground. Crew of 9 landed by Easington Rocket Brigade. Lifeboat out at 4 a.m. but so much sea did not get off.

May 10th   Lifeboat launch with Inspector and I went with them. First attempt a failure, second got off, rather heavy sea. Commander Carver here to tea after.

1924

Feb 8th   S.T. *Cortina* of Grimsby. Came ashore at Turmarr Bottom. Lifeboat and rocket brigade out, but crew would not leave the vessel. Lifeboat out again from 2 p.m. to 7:45 p.m. to assist with a coble to connect with tug etc.

March 29th Lifeboat practice and I went out with them. A choppy sea. George Stevenson made a bother before the launch.

April 26th Found damage had been done to lifeboat house by stone throwing.

Aug 5th Lifeboat practice and I went out. Very smooth.

Oct 23rd The *Viola* a motor drifter of Iceland, came ashore on fire about 300 yds south of road end. Crew of 5 saved by rocket brigade. Lifeboat summoned but not required.

Nov 27th The S.T. *Salacon* of Grimsby came ashore north of Dimlington at about 5 a.m. Snowing and very heavy sea. Our lifeboat took off 7 men and the rocket brigade 2 men.

Nov 30th S.T. *Isernia* ashore at Dimlington. Our lifeboat out, but a tug towed her off before it got there.

1925

Aug 1st Lifeboat launch and I went out with them. Sea smooth with rather a heavy roll outside, big shore waves that soaked us coming in. Two oars smashed and other damage. Box collection on beach by Violet and Jessie Nobbs. £1/17/-.

Aug 21st Latchet and 40ft flagpole fixed at lifeboat house.

1926

Feb 7th About 9 p.m. the S.T. *Rollo* of Grimsby came ashore off here. Lifeboat crew and rocket cart out, but she had got off again.

July 8th S.T. *Treasure* of Grimsby came ashore at the Old Hive at 10.50 p.m..

July 9th Lifeboat left at 1:15 a.m., but trawler had got off at 2:30 a.m. and gone.

1927

March 23rd Capt. Carver and Mr. Lewis (engineer) in Easington in morning to see about slipway for lifeboat.

Oct 21st New lifeboat slip begun.

Dec 2nd Lifeboat slip finished.

1928

April 12th Lifeboat practice with Capt. Carver and I went out with them.

Aug 6th Lifeboat launched. First attempt horses got among the clays and three or more came down, throwing their riders. Stanley Clubley being hurt. Boat became fixed and was released with much trouble. Second try we got off easily and I went with them.

1929

April 16th I wrote to Rev. Holt resigning the Chair and Membership of the Easington Lifeboat Committee.

April 17th I returned my key of the lifeboat house to Coxn. Branton.

Dec 17th Our lifeboat went to S.T. *Lucerne* ashore at Old Hive. Lifeboat out again at 9 p.m. to the S.T. *Bengal* ashore south of Holmpton.

1931

May 23rd   Lifeboat out at 1:30 a.m. to a ship ashore at Kilnsea Warren. Got off.

1933

April 2nd   Two steam trawlers ashore, Kilnsea and Dimlington. Lifeboat out.

May 30th   Lifeboat fittings sold by auction by F.Hill.

May 31st   Our lifeboat *Docea Chapman* taken to Patrington for London.

As will have been noticed, there is frequent mention of the rocket cart or rocket brigade in some of the reports of vessels in distress. This was a volunteer section of men that worked with the Board of Trade group of early coastguards. If called upon they would fire a rocket over the ship in distress, and then rig up a breeches buoy to haul, by means of ropes and pulleys, any mariners to the safety of the beach.

Fig. 49 The breeches buoy

Fig. 50 The Board of Trade Rocket Cart with crew

Fig. 51 Rocket crew and coastguards

Fig. 52 Preparing for a practice

Fig. 53 Rocket crew practice

Fig. 54 Firing the rocket

The following three photographs are not of Easington Rocket crew but are included to show the method of breeches buoy rescue

Fig. 55 Firing a rocket out to a ship

Fig. 56 Bringing a man ashore

Fig. 57 The rescued man sat in the breeches buoy

Although this now closes the chapter on the History of the
Easington Lifeboat it would be remiss of me not to chart the
remainder of the boat's life:

PART TWO

58

THE DOCEA CHAPMAN LIVES ON!!

(albeit under a different name)

DOCEA CHAPMAN
Ongoing

After the boat had left Easington and was taken on its horse-drawn carriage to Patrington railway station, the boat was transported to the RNLI store yard at Poplar in London on June 7th 1933, and there placed in the reserve fleet until 1st March 1938.

Due to a terrible disaster in 1938 when the St. Ives lifeboat went out to help a vessel the *Alba*, the lifeboat was totally wrecked on the rocks with a consequent heavy loss of life. Whilst waiting for a new lifeboat, the RNLI sent the Padstow second lifeboat to St. Ives to act as cover.

On 1st March 1938 the *Docea Chapman* was sent to Padstow No. 2 lifeboat station to act as temporary lifeboat until a motor lifeboat became available.

Fig. 58 Docea Chapman on slipway, Hawkers Cove, Padstow.
The Docea Chapman was never launched

It was whilst on service at Padstow that the boat was finally withdrawn from service and sold for £45 by the RNLI on February 28th 1939. A local man by the name of Mr. Barr bought the boat to use for fishing, but with the onset of World War II the boat was tied up and left for that period.

After the war had finished, work began on converting the boat. Stripping out the inside, raising the gunwales, fitting a 4 cylinder 'Kelvin' petrol/paraffin engine, a car steering wheel and a cable system on the aft whaleback, allowed the rudder to operate. She was also fitted with a mizzenmast and sail. When stripping out the boat, the owners described how well built it was and how difficult it was to dismantle. The hull was riveted every few inches so that the whole structure was stiff and strong. There was a deck that was divided into a honeycomb of flotation chambers between it and the bilge. Each chamber about one foot square held together with brass screws about four inches set into teak deck planks. They had never been opened since the boat was built around 1910. The screws were extremely difficult to remove and took a long time. Inside, the chambers were immaculate and glistened with their white leaded canvas linings. Also set in the deck were about 10/12 automatic scuppers to give the boat self-draining capability if breaking seas flooded it. These scuppers were about six inches in diameter with a one-way butterfly valve fitted to allow the water to flow out underneath the boat, but to prevent water from coming back into the boat as it pitched. There were also about ten more flap-type scuppers in the hull sides just below the gunwale. All these had to be removed to allow the conversion to be carried out. The boat was registered in Padstow and renamed *Kayandem* after Mr. Barr's two sons, Keith and Michael, who had assisted with the conversion. It was used for several years fishing along that part of the coast, then eventually was sold to a Mr. Tuman. After a while he in turn sold it on to a Mr. Tommy Morrisey. Mr. Morrisey added a second engine and foremast, also reshaping the interior and adding an enclosed wheelhouse up forward for added weather protection and also fitted a winch. He renamed the boat *Girl Maureen.*

Fig. 59 Girl Maureen ex Docea Chapman, early 1960s

Fig. 60 Girl Maureen, with a small wheelhouse forward, late 1960s

Thomas Morrisey used the boat for a number of years for fishing, until his retirement, when he sold the boat to a museum at Lynmouth in Devon. They completely stripped the boat and restored it to its original condition as a lifeboat. It was renamed *Louisa II* and went on display in its own building in Lynmouth.

This restoration was carried out to commemorate an epic event that took place at Lynmouth in Devon in 1899, by their lifeboat at the time, *Louisa*.

A brief description of that event follows:

On 12th January 1899, a large sailing ship, the *Forest Hall* was seen to be in distress in the Bristol Channel. Due to the ferocity of the weather and state of the sea it was impossible to launch the lifeboat from Lynmouth and, as the telegraph wires were down due to the intensity of the storm they could not get communication to another lifeboat station. So, they decided to take the lifeboat overland to a more sheltered area of coast and launch the boat there. The nearest available place was called Porlock Weir further up the coast. This involved dragging the lifeboat on its horse-drawn carriage up Countisbury Hill, which in parts has a 1 in 4 gradient, then on reaching the top travel was across the exposed area of Exmoor.

Fig. 61 A model of the Forest Hall

Fig. 62 Countisbury Hill in Devon

At one point they had to remove the lifeboat from its carriage, drag it by hand and horse for nearly a mile through a very narrow lane then put it back on its carriage to continue the journey down an even steeper hill with all its twists and turns, into the village of Porlock.

An advanced party had gone ahead to ensure the route was wide enough to accommodate the lifeboat and its carriage. This involved chopping down trees and knocking over stonewalls. They even had to knock a hole in a stone cottage to allow the passage of the lifeboat. They achieved this remarkable feat, covering a distance of some 15 miles through a night of atrocious weather conditions, across this wild and desolate part of the country, arriving at Porlock some 12 hours later and then launching to go to the aid of the vessel in distress.

Fig. 63 *An information board from the museum in Lynmouth,
although it wrongly states that the Docea Chapman was based at
Easington Co. Durham and should read Easington, East Yorkshire*

Fig. 64 *A model of the Louisa in the museum*

Fig .65 The ex Docea Chapman now renamed the Louisa ll on display in Lynmouth

Fig. 66 An interior view of the museum

It would appear that the museum closed around 2006, and the lifeboat has been put on display outside at Glen Lyn Gorge, Lynmouth.

Fig. 67 Docea Chapman in her new position

*The Bengal, one of the ships mentioned in the story that came
ashore south of Holmpton in 1929*

The Leonora ashore at Dimlington

*Two photos of a ship, name unknown, ashore at Easington
probably set alight on purpose*

Bibliography and Credits

We would like to acknowledge the following sources of information for various quotes in this publication.

Minutes of the RNLI Committee.
Easington Parish Council Minutes.
Memories of Mr. Jim Biglin.
Memories of Mr. Redvers Clubley.
Memories of Mr. Bob Wilson.
Diary extracts of Mr. Robert Walker.
The Hull Daily Mail, 5th May 1933.

I would like to thank Mr. Leo Chapman of Grimsby, a relation of the benefactor's family, for his loan of photographs and for information supplied. Thanks to Mrs. Stella Morris for permission to use extracts from Robert Walker's diary and photographs.

Grimsby Reference Library.

Mr. George Phillips, ex Hon. Sec. of Padstow Lifeboat station and Mr. John Francis, of the Lifeboat Enthusiast Society for photographs used.

Mr. Roy Benfell for assisting with information.

Also thanks to Mr. Walter Broom, Mr. John Broom, and Mr. Syd Rollinson for the loan of some of the photos used in this book.

Photographs taken in the Lighthouse Museum, Withernsea.

Photo from Mr. George de Boer.

The Spurn, Kilnsea and Easington Area Local Studies Group
(SKEALS) was formed in the summer
of 2006.

The group's aims are:
To bring together people interested in
local history, and support them in
sharing their knowledge and ideas.
To encourage research and the
recording of information about the area.
To disseminate information via events,
publications, a web site, and any other
means of communication.
*Easington Lifeboat a History 1913 –
1933* is a detailed story of the lifeboat
Docea Chapman from being originally stationed at Withernsea,
coming to Easington, together with the rest of its history to the
present day. This is the third publication from the Skeals group.
The group is researching a variety of topics of historical interest
relating to the area. Information on our activities and projects are
reported on our web page at http://www.skeals.co.uk, which is
updated frequently, and includes a wide range of material on our
area. Skeals has already carried out several projects including the
renovation of a historic plaque, work on some early grave-stones
formerly used as a path and now placed in Easington churchyard,
and the recording and photographing of gravestones. Exhibitions,
talks, and other public events are also part of our programme. We
welcome new members, both locally and from further afield. If
you are interested in taking an active part in SKEALS, or if you
have historical material, such as photographs, letters,
reminiscences and so on, that you think might be of interest, we
would love to hear from you. Our e-mail addresses are
skeals@btinternet.com and skealsgroup@hotmail.co.uk . For our
other publications see next two pages.

This is an illustrated history of Connor & Graham, a 20th-century bus company that served the Holderness community for 70 years from its headquarters in the village of Easington, near Spurn Point. Packed with photographs, anecdotes, lists of buses and staff, this book will be of interest to anyone who has been a passenger of Connor & Graham, has worked for them, is interested in bus history, or wants to know more about the South Holderness area. The book is written by Mike Welton, and published by SKEALS, the Spurn, Kilnsea and Easington Area Local Studies Group.

Over 100 pages in length with over 100 photographs, the book is for sale at only £6. It can be obtained from the author, tel. 01964 650265, email: mikewelton@lineone.net, or at local shops in the South Holderness area. Or see our web site at www.skeals.co.uk.

Memories of Spurn in the 1880s by George A. Jarratt (ISBN 978-0-9565048-1-4). A fascinating story related by someone who spent his childhood years at Spurn.

This insight into life at Spurn Point is the second publication by SKEALS, the Spurn, Kilnsea, and Easington Area Local Studies Group. It is the personal memories of George A. Jarratt, whose father was a lifeboatman at Spurn from 1883 until 1891. George was taken there when six months old, and spent his early childhood growing up in this remote and desolate location. He describes some of the problems of daily life on the peninsula as experienced by the adults, and the delights for a child of living in this unusual environment in the late Victorian period. Produced to coincide with the two-hundredth anniversary of a lifeboat at Spurn, the book is a new edition of an earlier publication. Mike Welton, the compiler has added many more photographs. The book, which has 39 pages, now contains some 44 photographs. The book is priced at only £5 (including post & packing £6). It can be obtained from Mike Welton, tel. 01964-650265, e-mail: mikewelton@lineone.net or at local shops in the South Holderness area. Or see our website at www.skeals.co.uk.

A donation of £1 will be given to the RNLI at Spurn for every copy sold.